RABBI KIRT A.
SCHNEIDER

THE
MYSTERY
of
DREAMS

CHARISMA
HOUSE

Library of Congress Cataloging-in-Publication Data:
An application to register this book for cataloging has been submitted to
the Library of Congress.
International Standard Book Number: 978-1-62999-866-4
E-book ISBN: 978-1-62999-867-1

20 21 22 23 24 — 987654321
Printed in the United States of America

CONTENTS

ACKNOWLEDGMENTS

To a degree we are all products of those around us who have invested into our lives. God often uses others to impart something of Himself to us. With this in mind, I want to thank my wife, Cynthia. And it goes without saying that, as always, I thank and praise the Lord! Baruch HaShem!

INTRODUCTION

IN THE EARLY 1980s, I was living in northeast Georgia, and my wife and I had a little beagle puppy. We built a fence in the backyard for the puppy to play in while we were gone, and at some point he dug a hole under the fence and got out of the yard.

The puppy had a collar with our phone number on it, but after he had been gone for about two months, I thought he was gone for good. Then one night I had a dream that we'd found him. I wasn't sure what to make of the dream because, as I said, I didn't think we'd ever see our puppy again. But the next day I got a call from a farmer who lived eight miles away saying he had found our dog. I picked our puppy up that day.

God had supernaturally shown me the future in my dream. And though that wasn't the first time God had spoken to me through a dream (I came to faith in Yeshua because of a dream), the experience caused me to start regularly writing my dreams down because I realized that God wanted to frequently communicate with me in my dreams.

In the more than thirty years since then, God has spoken to me powerfully through dreams. And I have written this book with one key purpose in mind: to help you see that God wants to speak to you in your dreams too.

God has always spoken to His children through dreams. In the Tanakh (Old Testament), God used dreams to

- reveal to Abraham His covenant for the birth of a people and nation (Gen. 15:12–16);

- convey to Jacob the inheritance He planned to give his descendants (Gen. 28:10–22);

- show Joseph a glimpse of his future (Gen. 37:5–11);

- prompt Pharaoh to release Joseph from prison, positioning Joseph to fulfill his destiny (Gen. 40–41);

- encourage Solomon in his role as a prophet and king of Israel (1 Kings 3:5–15); and

- warn Daniel of future kingdoms, a coming war, and events surrounding the second coming of the Messiah (Dan. 7).

In the Brit Chadashah (New Testament), God used dreams to

- direct Joseph four consecutive times: to remove his fear of taking Mary as his wife (Matt. 1:20–21), to instruct him to flee Bethlehem for Egypt (Matt. 2:13), to tell him it was safe to return to Israel (Matt. 2:19–20), and to warn him to take his family to Galilee instead of Judea (Matt. 2:22);

- speak to Pontius Pilate's wife about the innocence of Jesus (Matt. 27:19); and

- direct Paul where to go as he traveled while spreading the gospel (Acts 16:9).

A pivotal scripture we will closely examine is from Acts 2, where Peter quotes the prophet Joel:

> And it shall come to pass in the last days, says God, that I will pour out of My Spirit on all flesh; your sons and your daughters shall prophesy, your young men shall see visions, your old men shall dream dreams.
>
> —ACTS 2:17, NKJV

Peter was speaking on the day of Pentecost, after the Holy Spirit had come upon Jesus' followers. He informed the gathered crowd that the disciples were not drunk with wine as they supposed but were instead filled with the Holy Spirit. We will study this vital connection between the words of Joel, written some eight hundred years earlier, and the apostle Peter's sermon, as they point to God's desire to advance His kingdom through dreams—which have been given to His people across millennia, up to this present day.

God indeed still speaks today and wants to speak to you in your dreams. Notice that both Peter at Pentecost in Acts 2 and the Old Testament prophet Joel (Joel 2:28) talk about three manifestations of the Holy Spirit: prophecy, visions, and dreams. While we will touch on all three, my main focus will be on dreams.

The difference between a dream and a vision is that visions happen while we are awake, and dreams take place while we sleep. Prophecy is speaking by inspiration of the

Holy Spirit or hearing a word that has been spoken to you by inspiration of the Holy Spirit.

God gave us the Holy Spirit at Pentecost so He could speak to us directly through these three manifestations. Of course, God also speaks to us constantly through His Word, other people, life's circumstances, nature, and so forth. We don't serve a God who no longer speaks, but a loving, intimate Father who wants to communicate with us, including while we dream.

For the purpose of this book, when I use the word *dream*, I am talking specifically about God's desire to speak to you while you are asleep—not about your goals, desires, and future hopes.

You may "dream" of one day visiting Europe, buying a house, or having children (or grandchildren). And while those types of dreams are admirable and important, this is not what I mean. Instead, I am talking about dreams in the night.

You may be thinking, "But Rabbi, I never remember my dreams!" Many people struggle to remember their dreams, while others seem to remember every dream they had from the night before. You know the type: they show up at work (or at the breakfast table) and share very specific details of the dream they had the previous night. If you are a "non-dreamer," it can actually be kind of annoying to listen to someone else's amazing dream experience! You may think, "Why don't I ever dream like that?"

But consider this: It has been scientifically proven that we *all* dream.[1] The problem isn't *if* we dream, then, but *how* to remember what we dream. God not only wants you to remember your dreams, He also wants to breathe words of revelation into your spirit as you sleep—revelation that will propel you into God's purpose for your life.

Jesus tells us that His sheep—that's us, you and me—hear His voice. (See John 10:14–15.) He does not say, "My sheep only hear My voice when they are awake." If God so loved the world that He gave His only Son as a sacrifice for our sins (John 3:16), doesn't it make sense that He would speak to us in our sleep? Currently the average life expectancy in the United States is 78.6 years.[2] If we sleep for nearly one-third of that time, it means we have between twenty-six and twenty-seven years of sleep time to hear *even more* from God!

It's important to point out that not all dreams are from God. The enemy tries to use dreams to distract and harass us. So it's important to recognize the difference between a godly dream and one that is not from God. As we discuss how to discern the difference, we will also touch on the discipline of interpretation—understanding the meaning and purpose of dreams.

As followers of Yeshua (Jesus in Hebrew) we rely not on our own understanding but upon the Word of God. You will be impressed by how often God uses dreams over and over in both the Tanakh and the Brit Chadashah. Throughout these chapters I will provide scriptural evidence that God has a long-standing, consistent practice of speaking to His children while they sleep.

We will also discuss the different ways in which the Ruach HaKodesh (Holy Spirit) wants to use the dreams that God will give to you. As you fine-tune your ability to remember, write down, and interpret your dreams, God will use this new level of revelation to propel you into the destiny He has designed for you.

Take heart if you are one of those people I mentioned previously who does not remember his or her dreams. Throughout these pages I will walk with you to help you break off whatever may be blocking you from hearing from God as you sleep. Together we will study His Word to gain insights that will help you hear and understand God's voice when He speaks to you in your sleep. As a result, you will discover how God uses dreams to give

- direction for your life,

- encouragement in your walk,

- insight into key events or situations,

- warnings about impending crises or other harmful issues,

- preparation for a coming change or major life shift,

- guidance to launch you into your destiny, and

- direction to bring about your sanctification.

I have structured the book so that the first section contains teaching and instruction on the above seven points. Then, as you can see as you leaf through the pages, I provide ample room for you to journal about the dreams you receive from God. In other words, we will lay a biblical foundation for hearing from God through dreams, and then apply the revelation God gives to you.

God has often used dreams to speak to me during the night. If you, too, are hearing from God in your dreams, my hope is that this book will help you to not only hone your ability to remember and interpret your dreams but also to use them to fulfill God's will for your life in an even more effective way.

And if you are a person who has never experienced a prophetic dream (i.e., a dream given by the Holy Spirit), my hope is that the teachings here will awaken you to hear God's voice in your sleep.

As you read these words, may you move into a powerful season of revelation where you more clearly recognize, capture, and use your God-given dreams.

PART I

UNDERSTANDING AND INTERPRETING YOUR DREAMS

CHAPTER 1

GOD STILL SPEAKS THROUGH DREAMS

I CAME TO FAITH supernaturally in 1978 through a vision in the night. I was twenty years old, and I was awakened from my sleep at three thirty in the morning. Suddenly I was aware that something supernatural was happening, and Jesus appeared to me.

The dream was in vivid color. Jesus appeared on the cross, and a ray of red light came through the sky and beamed down on His head. There were people in the distance looking at Him, just as I read about later in the New Testament. And when I saw that ray of red light come down on Yeshua's head, I knew God was saying to me, "Jesus is the way to Me."

At the time, I knew very little about Yeshua. I was raised in a Jewish home, attended synagogue on all the high holy days, went to Hebrew school, and was bar mitzvahed at thirteen. Yeshua appearing to a Jewish kid in his Cleveland bedroom isn't a typical occurrence—but it happened to me. And that dream, that vision of the night, changed my life.

No one has to convince me that God still speaks to people today in their dreams. I am a walking, living example of how He continues to communicate with His children. Mine was a completely natural encounter with our supernatural God.

In the forty-plus years since that night in 1978 I have found that the people who seem to be most excited about Yeshua are those who experience God's activity, presence, and supernatural gifts in their lives. In contrast, some people think that all we can do in this life is study the Bible, go to church, and then wait to die so we can experience God in heaven. But nothing could be further from the truth.

God is here, He is now, and He communicates with His people! King David knew this. In Psalm 27, David said that if he didn't believe he could experience the goodness of the Lord in the land of the living, meaning in his present life, he would have fainted (v. 13). And one of the primary ways God communicates with us is through our dreams at night.

As my wife, Cynthia, can tell you, during our thirty-six years of marriage God has spoken to me over and over through dreams. As a couple, we have made some remarkable decisions because the Lord spoke to us in dreams. Just as importantly, we have seen the fruit of those dreams in our lives.

As my wife and I have sought to better understand our dreams, we've seen time and again where the Lord has spoken and truly guided our steps to keep us right on track with His will for our lives. This gift of dreams is not just for us. It is for you too. This book will examine scriptures that show us how God speaks through dreams—and that He still uses them to speak to us today.

AS IT WAS SPOKEN THROUGH THE PROPHET JOEL

As we explore God's Word, I want to begin with the Hebrew prophet Joel. Read the following passage slowly, as these are the verses Peter quoted on the day of Pentecost some eight centuries later:

> Thus you will know that I am in the midst of Israel, and that I am the LORD your God, and there is no other; and My people will never be put to shame. It will come about after this that I will pour out My Spirit on all mankind; and your sons and daughters will prophesy, your old men will dream dreams, your young men will see visions.
>
> —JOEL 2:27–28

In these scriptures the Lord was prophesying through Joel about what He was going to do in a last-days movement by His Spirit. God was specifically referring to that future time when the Holy Spirit would be given to His church.

Keep this passage from Joel in mind as we fast-forward to first-century Jerusalem, fifty days after the resurrection. We read in Acts 2, "When the day of Pentecost had come, they were all together in one place" (v. 1).

When we think of Pentecost, we think of the giving of God's Spirit that took place two thousand years ago as the believers were gathered together in Jerusalem. But understand that when those first believers were gathered, they were thinking about what happened at Mount Sinai fifteen hundred years earlier, on that exact day.

In Judaism the Hebrew word for this particular Jewish holy day is *Shavuot*. The New Testament was written in Greek, so the equivalent word is *Pentecost*. *Shavuot* means "weeks," because in the Torah there was a special day celebrated seven "weeks" and a day after Passover: the Feast of Weeks, or Shavuot. We simply say Pentecost in the Greek, which means fifty, because seven weeks plus a day equals fifty.

Christians often think that Pentecost is a New Testament holiday, when in fact Pentecost is rooted in the Torah. So these new believers were gathered together in Jerusalem as the Jewish people had been doing for fifteen hundred years, ever since God gave the Law (i.e., the Torah, the first five books of the Old Testament) to Moses atop Mount Sinai.

As they were gathered in the Upper Room, the followers of Yeshua were thinking of how fifteen centuries earlier the Lord revealed Himself in glory on top of Mount Sinai and then wrote His law on tablets of stone. So while they were commemorating this event, suddenly the same God who appeared at Mount Sinai manifested Himself again in glory. But this time God did it in tongues of fire, and He wrote His law not upon stone but upon their hearts.

When the Holy Spirit fell at Pentecost, observers did not know what was going on. The power of God's glory was so strong that those looking on thought the disciples were drunk. In fact, the believers were so overwhelmed by the weight of the Ruach HaKodesh that they could not stand up straight.

The events of Acts 2 mirrored what happened to the priests in the first temple during the time of Solomon. They had brought the ark of the covenant of the Lord to its place in the inner sanctuary of the temple, called the Most Holy Place. First Kings 8 says that when the priests "came out of the Holy Place, the cloud filled the house of the LORD, so that the priests could not continue to minister because of the cloud, for the glory of the LORD filled the house of the LORD" (vv. 10–11, MEV).

Sound familiar? The same type of phenomenon that happened at the time of Solomon was happening at Pentecost! And then Peter stood up and said, "These men are not drunk. What you're seeing is what Joel prophesied." (See Acts 2:15–16). Peter then quoted the passage from Joel 2 that we read previously.

So, with that in mind, let's continue reading in Acts 2:

> When the day of Pentecost had come, they were all together in one place. And suddenly there came from heaven a noise like a violent rushing wind, and it filled the whole house where they were sitting. And there appeared to them tongues as of fire distributing themselves, and they rested on each one of them. And they were all filled with the Holy Spirit [in Hebrew we say the Ruach HaKodesh—the holy breath of life] and began to speak with other tongues, as the Spirit was giving them utterance.
>
> Now there were Jews living in Jerusalem, devout men from every nation under heaven. And when this sound occurred, the crowd came together, and were bewildered because each one of them was hearing them speak in his own language. They were amazed and astonished, saying, "Why, are not all these who are speaking Galileans? And how is it that we each hear them in our own language to which we were born?"…They all continued in amazement and great perplexity, saying to one another, "What does this mean?" But others were mocking and saying, "They are full of sweet wine."
>
> —ACTS 2:1–8, 12

Now notice what Peter says:

> But Peter, taking his stand with the eleven, raised his voice and declared to them: "Men of Judea and all you who live in Jerusalem, let this be known

to you and give heed to my words. For these men are not drunk, as you suppose, for this is only the third hour of the day; but this is what was spoken of through the prophet Joel."

—ACTS 2:14–16

Again, Peter is quoting from Joel, as we discussed earlier. He says:

"And it shall be in the last days," God says, "That I will pour forth of My Spirit on all mankind; and your sons and your daughters shall *prophesy*, and your young men shall see *visions*, and your old men shall dream *dreams*; even on My bondslaves, both men and women, I will in those days pour forth of My Spirit and they shall prophesy."

—ACTS 2:17–18, EMPHASIS ADDED

Both Peter and Joel say the same thing relating to prophecy, visions, and dreams—that they are three manifestations of the Holy Spirit. Each is distinct, and they are for today.

- Dreams are thoughts, images, and words we receive during sleep that come from God and provide direction for one's life.

- Visions are much like dreams, but they happen while we are awake.

- Prophecy is speaking by inspiration of the Holy Spirit.

To be clear, it's not just young men who have visions and old men who have dreams. (See Acts 2:17–18.) Peter is speaking about all classes of people. After the outpouring of the Holy Spirit, all God's people would be able to experience these three manifestations of the Spirit.

The key point Peter is making is that God still speaks to people today, and more so now that the Holy Spirit has been given. All followers of Yeshua have the opportunity to see in the Spirit and receive revelation from the Ruach HaKodesh through their dreams.

Before we begin our study of dreams, I want to briefly discuss the other two manifestations mentioned by Joel and Peter—prophecy and visions—because both are blessings or benefits of the Holy Spirit available to all believers. First, let's talk about prophecy.

PROPHECY

The Hebrew word for *prophecy* is *naba'*. And the most elementary definition of this term is to speak by inspiration of the Spirit.[1] Sometimes we make prophecy very mysterious and overly complicated. A prophetic word, however, does not always have to be delivered with the words, "Thus saith the Lord."

To speak by inspiration of the Lord can be something as profoundly simple as being prompted in your heart to reach out and call your mother. God may inspire you to just ask her how she's doing. Or a prophetic inspiration might be when you feel led to contact a friend and tell them that you love them and are praying for them. That, my friend, is prophecy in its simplest form, when these acts and words spoken are by the inspiration of the Ruach Elohim (Spirit of God).

Of course, there are many different levels of prophecy. A prophetic word can get very deep in terms of God giving you secrets about a person's life. For example, sometime back I gave an altar call during a special Yom Kippur (Day of Atonement) service about the need to forgive in order to experience the Lord's forgiveness. There were many visitors who had come forward to receive ministry. As I made my way down the line of those who had come to receive prayer, I came to a middle-aged woman whom I had never met before in my life.

As I stood before her, I intuited the Holy Spirit telling me that she had a problem with her sister. So I gently said to this woman whom I had never met, "Are you having a problem in your relationship with your sister?" Immediately upon my saying that to her, she started crying. I had spoken directly into her heart through a prophetic word. She knew I could never have known that on my own. So when I asked that question, she knew that God was speaking to her, and it overwhelmed her to know how close God was to her and that He loved her enough to speak to her with such intimate knowledge.

I have seen people who did not yet know Yeshua receive these kinds of prophetic words, and as a result their hearts were opened to receive God's love and salvation.

Let me give you an example of a prophecy I once received. Years ago when my daughters first started driving, I became panic-stricken every time they got in the car. This was more than just a nervous parent worried about his new teenage driver.

What really set it off was that one of my daughters was involved in two separate car accidents. The accidents happened just a few days apart, and one of them could have been very bad. Thankfully, no one was seriously injured. But the combination of those back-to-back accidents put me in a state of fear whenever one of my daughters got behind the wheel.

One day, both daughters were walking out the door, and my sixteen-year-old at the time had just gotten her driver's license. I was afraid for their lives, and I didn't know what to do. After they left, I was so overwhelmed by fear that I decided to take a nap in the middle of the afternoon, which is very unlike me. While I was sleeping, I had a dream where I saw myself crying out to the congregation that I was pastoring at the time. I said, "*Pray for me. I need you to pray for me.*" Then I woke up.

As soon as I awoke, I noticed that I had received a voicemail from a woman in my congregation. She had called while I was asleep having this dream where I was crying out to my congregation, "*Pray for me.*" In her voicemail message she said, "Rabbi, I don't know what's going on, but I want you to know that the Lord just put you right in front of my face." And she said, "Rabbi, I'm praying for you."

That was prophecy. She literally called me and said, "Rabbi, I'm praying for you"—the exact same words I was calling out in my dream. In fact, she might have been prompted to call me and say, "I'm praying for you," at the very moment I was having the dream asking my congregation for prayer. When that woman called and spoke to me by the inspiration of the Spirit, it assured me that God was with me, loved me, heard me, and could be trusted. Receiving that prophetic word released me from my fears.

As followers of Yeshua, we all have the ability to prophesy. Sometimes you can speak by prophetic inspiration and you won't even know it. Have you ever had someone tell you well after the fact that God spoke to them through you? Perhaps it's years later and that person says, "No one knew what I was going through, but God used you to encourage me." You were being led to speak by the inspiration of the Holy Spirit, which is one of the effects of having God's Spirit poured out on us.

VISIONS

The second benefit or blessing we experience because God's Spirit has been poured out on us is that we see visions. Both Acts and the Book of Joel reflect this, saying, "Your young men shall see visions" (Joel 2:28; Acts 2:17).

A vision is a Holy Spirit–inspired image or impression that a person receives when he or she is awake. Now, when you think of seeing visions from God, you may think of the kinds of visions described in the Bible. For example, in Isaiah 6 the prophet was caught up in the spirit world and saw a majestic, awe-inspiring image of God's holiness. Isaiah saw the Lord on His throne, and it was so overwhelming that he fell to the ground and cried out, "Woe is me" (Isa. 6:5).

The prophet Ezekiel had a dramatic vision of God's majesty, love, and glory in the form of four creatures that each had four faces. (See Ezekiel 1:4–28.) And of course, John in the Book of Revelation was called up to heaven and witnessed the Lamb on the throne and the creatures worshipping God. Indeed, the entire Book of Revelation was a prophetic vision that God gave to the apostle John, who was told to write down what was revealed and send it to the seven churches of Asia Minor. Like Isaiah and Ezekiel, John was totally overwhelmed by the vision God gave him.

But I want you to know, beloved, that most visions God gives His people are very subtle. They're typically not the dramatic visions that we read about in the Bible. Instead, most visions are gentle—so much so that if you are not paying attention, you might miss them.

When God spoke to Elijah at Horeb, for example, He did so quietly:

> The LORD said, "Go out and stand on the mountain in the presence of the LORD, for the LORD Is about to pass by." Then a great and powerful wind tore the mountains apart and shattered the rocks before the LORD, but the LORD was not in the wind. After the wind there was an earthquake, but the LORD was not in the earthquake. After the earthquake came a fire, but the LORD was not in the fire. And after the fire came a gentle whisper.
> —1 KINGS 19:11–12, NIV

You see, generally God speaks not in an earthquake or a violent fire but in the gentle wind. For instance, when He gives you a vision, you may see a simple picture in your mind. A picture is worth a thousand words.

That is what happened to me many years ago while I was leading a prayer meeting. I looked at a man sitting across from me, and all of a sudden I saw a simple picture in my mind. It was very subtle. If I had not been paying attention and conscious of the fact that the impression might be from the Lord, I may have missed it. I saw a hammer coming down on this man's head, and I said, "I don't know if this means anything, but I just saw a picture in my mind of a hammer coming down on your head."

He said, "Rabbi, I just found out today that I am getting sued." When I shared my vision with him, he was very encouraged and knew that God saw him, cared, and loved him. Because I was able to receive God's revelation through this vision in the Spirit, this man realized the Lord knew exactly what was going on in his life and that God would see him through it.

We've only just touched on the blessings of prophecy and visions long enough to define them. But as I have said, what I really want to focus on in this book is communication from the Lord we can receive through our dreams. Again, to be clear, I'm not talking about having a dream for your life (i.e., a goal or desire). Rather, I am talking about supernatural presentations that come to us by the Holy Spirit when we're sleeping. Through such prophetic dreams the Ruach Elohim is able to reveal to us wisdom and direction from God.

I've said it before, but it bears repeating: whether you know it or not, you dream. And I believe that as you read this book, God is going to open you up to better receive from Him in your sleep. I believe He's going to begin the process of eliminating whatever might be preventing you from hearing Him speak to you through your dreams. And as a result, you are going to be more clearly guided in your life and directed by His Spirit.

In the next chapter we will discuss how to improve your ability to hear God in your dreams.

CHAPTER 2

HEARING GOD IN YOUR DREAMS

THE QUESTION IS not whether God is speaking today, but whether or not we have ears to hear Him. As we discovered in the first chapter, God spoke to His people in the Old Testament in much the same ways He did in the New Testament. He has always used prophecy, dreams, and visions to communicate with His children.

We established that God still uses dreams in the night to communicate with us. The real question is, Are you hearing what God wants to say to you, and how well are you hearing Him?

EARS TO HEAR

Several times in the Gospels Yeshua says, "He who has ears to hear, let him hear." (See Matthew 11:15; 13:9, 43; Mark 4:9; and Luke 8:8; 14:35.) Of course, Yeshua wasn't questioning whether or not His audience had ears that audibly heard; rather, He was challenging His listeners to open their spiritual ears to both hear and understand His words.

Like signal bars on a cell phone, our "reception" of what God is saying to us can vary. If we are in a "dead zone" (distracted, disinterested, or otherwise not in a place of good reception), we won't be able to hear what God is trying to tell us.

At the beginning of Revelation, John is told to write down what the Spirit is saying to him about the seven churches in Asia Minor. He says, "Blessed is he who reads and those who hear the words of the prophecy, and heed the things which are written in it; for the time is near" (Rev. 1:3). It is not enough for us to simply *read* the words; we must *hear* them. In each letter John uses the same admonishment: "He who has an ear, let him hear what the Spirit says to the churches." (See Revelation 2–3.)

Why is this important to us today? Because God is speaking individually and specifically to His people through the Ruach HaKodesh, who has been personally given to each believer. The fact is that God is always speaking, but we sometimes struggle to hear Him. For this reason, we need to pray that Father God will strengthen us to hear and quicken our awareness to be able to discern His voice. My goal is to help you increase your spiritual acuity so you can hear and intuit the Lord all around you.

We don't have to wait to go to heaven to hear from God. Perhaps that statement alone is a revelation to you. Maybe you were taught to believe that God is in heaven, you are down here on the earth, and the lines of communication were cut thousands of years ago. But not only is that false; it's not biblical. Yeshua, who indeed is our Good Shepherd not only when we go to heaven but also while we are here on the earth, says, "My sheep hear My voice, and I know them, and they follow Me" (John 10:27).

When the followers of Yeshua were given the Holy Spirit in Acts 2, He came upon them as tongues of fire:

> There appeared to them tongues as of fire, being distributed and resting on each of them, and they were

all filled with the Holy Spirit and began to speak in
other tongues, as the Spirit enabled them to speak.
—Acts 2:3–4, mev

Why did the Holy Spirit manifest Himself as tongues
of fire? A tongue is a speaking oracle. Now that the Spirit
has been poured out, we will hear God speak to us by
His Spirit. Tongues are for speaking, just as ears are for
hearing.

This is why it is important to hear the Lord when He
speaks to us through the "tongue" of the Holy Spirit. He
speaks to us, of course, by the Word of God. The Spirit
of God places weight on the Word and imparts it to our
spirit. But God can also speak to us through other people,
through events or circumstances, and even through
nature. It is also very important to realize He speaks by
divine intuition, meaning that by simply being sensitive to
the Holy Spirit within us, we can discern His voice.

GOD STILL GUIDES THROUGH DREAMS

Despite the many ways the Lord speaks to us, we must
remember that He also speaks to us powerfully through
dreams. The Bible is the foundation for all faith and practice in our walk with God. But the Ruach HaKodesh can
speak to us about specific details that sometimes the Word
of God doesn't address. For example, the Bible doesn't tell
us whether we should move to a certain city, make a particular investment, or marry a specific person. But God
wants to speak to us about the details of our lives, and
sometimes He'll do that through a dream at night.

Am I saying you should abandon the Bible and only
seek revelation from dreams? Absolutely not! What I am

saying is that while the Bible is our standard for living, at times the Holy Spirit will speak to us through dreams.

In fact, when we survey the Scriptures, we find that one of the most common ways the Lord speaks to His people is through dreams. From the very beginning of the Bible (e.g., with Abraham in Genesis) all the way to the end of the New Testament (with John in Revelation), the Lord spoke to His people as they slept.

If He did it then, is He not still doing it today? Of course He is, because God is the same yesterday, today, and forever (Heb. 13:8). In fact, we should expect Him to be speaking *more* to us today through our dreams, because it's one of the blessings we are given when we receive the Spirit of Elohim.

In Acts 2, Peter confirms and verifies God's use of dreams both in his day and in the future when he says, your old men *will* dream dreams (Joel 2:28; Acts 2:17). God has not rescinded the gift; dreams are still for today.

To have a dream from the Lord is when He comes to us in our sleep and communicates with us visually, audibly, or both. He communicates to us in order to reveal His will for our lives.

God-given dreams can warn us, encourage us, or speak to us about the future. Over the course of these chapters we are going to explore the various types of dreams that we see illustrated in Scripture. I will also share personal stories of different types of dreams I have had to show how God has directed my life through dreams.

Scripture illustrates how God uses dreams to precisely guide His sons and daughters. We see a vivid example of this in Acts 16, where God used a dream (which Scripture sometimes calls a vision of the night) to give Paul, Timothy, and Silas detailed guidance during their travels through Asia Minor:

> They went through the region of Phrygia and Galatia and were forbidden by the Holy Spirit to speak the word in Asia. When they came near Mysia, they tried to go into Bithynia, but the Spirit did not allow them. So they passed by Mysia and went down to Troas. During the night a vision appeared to Paul: A man of Macedonia stood and pleaded with him, saying, "Come over to Macedonia and help us." After he had seen the vision, immediately we sought to go into Macedonia, concluding that the Lord had called us to preach the gospel to them.
> —ACTS 16:6–10, MEV

This passage shows God carefully directing the travelers' steps through dreams and prophecy. Later on, Paul traveled to Corinth, and once again God visited him in a dream, saying:

> Do not be afraid, but speak and do not be silent. For I am with you, and no one shall attack you and hurt you, for I have many people in this city.
> —ACTS 18:9–10, MEV

Paul had ears to hear, and because of that, God spoke to him often. As Matthew 13:12 says, "For whoever has, to him more shall be given." Notice that in the two previous examples from Acts, Paul received a warning, direction, and encouragement through his dreams.

To give you another example of how God uses dreams to guide us, I want to share a story of what happened to me years ago when I was pastoring a congregation. One night

I had a dream in which a group of people was standing in a circle throwing a ball to one another. I walked up to the circle to join in the game, and immediately—*bam!*—someone threw the ball to me.

But since I had just arrived, I didn't know what game they were playing, so I didn't know what to do with the ball. I just stood there because I didn't understand the point of the game or the rules. So I looked at the person on my left and said, "What am I supposed to do? I don't know how to play this game."

The person just looked at me without responding. Then I turned to the person on my right and said, "I don't understand what I'm supposed to do with the ball. I've got the ball, but I don't know what to do with it." He wouldn't tell me. I became so frustrated that I put the ball down and just walked out of the circle.

The dream then changed to a new scene where I was standing in a shopping mall. In the dream I was still completely self-absorbed and frustrated about what had happened in the game where I didn't know the rules and no one would explain them to me. I was walking through the mall thinking about this and upset about the whole thing.

As I was walking, I saw someone that I knew. So I walked up to this person and said in frustration, "I was just in this situation where people were playing this game." I explained the whole situation to this person in the mall and what had just happened to me. And the person said, "If you had been aware of what was going on with the rest of the people in the circle with you, you would have known who to throw the ball to and when."

Just then I woke up and was really disturbed by the dream I'd just had. I knew for certain that the Lord had spoken to me, but I didn't understand the dream. As I lay awake in bed, I wondered what the whole thing meant.

Slowly the Holy Spirit began to cause me to intuitively understand the dream. And what He said to me was this: "I was showing you how I want you to lead and conduct the services where you are pastoring. I don't want you to go in and have such a rigid format for the way the service is going to go. It's so rigid that you don't leave room for Me to speak to you. Rather than being so rigid in the way you're orchestrating the service, I want you to feel what's going on with everybody in the sanctuary. I want you to feel what I'm doing with the people, and then you'll know what to do with the ball. You'll know how to lead the services better. You'll be more in tune with what I'm doing in the present moment rather than missing what I'm doing because you're so fixated on following your agenda."

That one dream changed the way I ministered. From that day on I tried to discern what the Holy Spirit was doing during our services. I was less hung up on my agenda or how I thought the service was supposed to flow. That dream helped me tune in to the congregation; it helped me listen to the Lord and flow in His anointing instead of being locked into my own ideas of what the service should look and feel like.

That dream was one of many that showed me God can speak very intimately and specifically to me during my dreams at night.

Tuning In to Your Dreams

I want to look at a passage of Scripture in the Book of Job. As you may recall, many of Job's counselors thought he was a fool for remaining faithful to God after experiencing so many hardships. For their disdain, they were rebuked by God. However, one of his counselors, Elihu, was not rebuked by HaShem (God). Listen to what Elihu said:

> For God speaks once, yes twice, yet man does not perceive it. In a dream, in a vision of the night, when deep sleep falls upon men, in slumber on their beds, then He opens the ears of men, and seals their instruction, that He might turn aside man from his purpose, and conceal pride from man. He keeps back his soul from the pit, and his life from perishing by the sword.
>
> —JOB 33:14–18, MEV

So what is Elihu saying? God is speaking once, twice, but people aren't noticing. When is God speaking? Elihu says it's in their dreams. His message is as timely for you today as it was for Job thousands of years ago: God is speaking to you in your dreams, but you may not be paying attention. You might be missing out on so much of what God wants to say because you don't even have an awareness that He is speaking to you in your sleep. Or if you do have a vague awareness, you are not doing anything to benefit from those dreams.

We will be able to more clearly and powerfully benefit from "God dreams" as we do the following.

- **Ask Him to speak.** Have you ever prayed before bedtime that God would visit you in your dreams? If not, now is the time to start.

- **Capture His words.** Yes, asking God to speak to us in our dreams is vital, but the

next step is just as important: capturing the
message that God is giving to us.

- **Write it down.** A critical part of capturing
  your dreams is writing them down. (In the
  final chapter we will go into more detail
  about how to do this and why this is so
  important.)

- **Pray for confirmation.** Ask the Lord for
  discernment and confirmation that the
  dream is indeed from Him. God will be
  faithful to confirm whether He is the source
  of the dream. (We will discuss the sources
  of our dreams in the next chapter.)

- **Pray to understand the dream.** After you
  capture your dream and confirm that it is of
  God, you need to then interpret its meaning.
  Why did the Lord show you what He did?
  What does He want you to do with the
  information from the dream?

- **Enter into alignment.** When you confirm
  the dream and interpret its meaning, it then
  becomes your responsibility to come into
  agreement with God regarding its purpose.
  Ask yourself, How does God want to use the
  dream to deepen my intimacy with Him or
  move me into a new level of ministry, and
  what must I do in response?

As you pursue these steps and begin to access and act upon your dreams, you will hear God rather than miss Him.

I love what King David said in Psalm 16 about the way the Lord ministered to him through his dreams at night:

> I will bless the LORD who has counseled me; indeed, my mind instructs me in the night.
>
> —PSALM 16:7

What a blessing to know and understand that God is working in our lives as we sleep. We face so many challenges that we need God's help to solve. There are so many decisions that we need to make, and so often we don't know what the right choice is. To know that God is helping us to navigate life, to overcome, and to make the right decisions by speaking to us in our sleep is deeply intimate. HaShem wants to remove any and all barriers that might hinder our minds from receiving His love so we can be like David and receive His counsel in the night.

As you develop your spiritual acuity to capture and act upon the dreams God gives you, He will clearly guide you in your pursuit of His plan for your life (i.e., your sanctification—your growth and maturity as a believer).

In Yeshua's name, I pray that your ears will be opened so you will receive more from Elohim than ever before.

CHAPTER 3

WHERE DREAMS COME FROM

Though I have been a believer in Yeshua for forty-plus years, it wasn't until about thirty years ago that I started to experience the supernatural in my life on a regular basis. As I entered into a deeper experience with the supernatural presence of God, I learned the hard way that not all supernatural phenomena—such as dreams and visions—are from God. In fact, the opposite is true: some things that are supernatural are not from God at all.

A common question I often hear is, "How do I know when a dream is from God?" It's a vital question because sometimes it is difficult to know what type of dream you are having. In fact, there are three sources of our dreams:

1. dreams from our natural mind

2. dreams from the enemy

3. dreams from God

In this chapter we will explore these three different types of dreams and how to tell them apart. We will also explore why God uses a method as mysterious as dreams to communicate to His children.

UNDERSTANDING THE SOURCE

The mistake I made early on was thinking that everything supernatural happening in my life was from the Lord. Because of that, I fell on my face; I made mistakes. The Lord had to take me through a time when He trained me and helped me develop discernment. Again, I think of the word *acuity*: God had to hone my spiritual acuity to discern what was from Him and what was not.

As you develop the ability to perceive God dreams, it will refine your walk with Him and align your steps so that you can live in tune with what He's speaking about. The more experience you get and the more mature you become, the better able you'll be to perceive which dreams are from your natural mind, which dreams are from the enemy, and which dreams are from God.

I would say that in my own life, most of the dreams I have are simply the result of my natural mind processing life's events, emotions, and experiences. A lot of the dreams we have at night are just the mind still dealing with things that we have experienced in our lives as human beings.

For example, my wife, Cynthia, handles so many responsibilities—from serving in the ministry to taking care of our home to being a wife, mother, and grandmother—that she feels at times like the work is never done. As a result of this, Cynthia will sometimes have dreams where the overall feeling is that she can't catch up. I know this is a common feeling among people who have to multitask, especially women.

We also may still be processing in our dreams things that happened in our lives many years ago. For example, people who fought in wars may still dream of being on the battlefield years and years after the literal experience.

In addition to having dreams as a result of our natural processing of life's events, emotions, and experiences, we also at times have dreams that come from the enemy. Mark my words: we are living in a spiritual environment. Even as we live in a physical environment with the sun or clouds, warm air or cold air, rain or dry times, so we exist in a spiritual climate as well. And part of living here on the earth and successfully navigating our lives in HaShem is coming to the realization that there are dark spiritual forces in our environment that can affect us while we are asleep and awake.

Some dreams are the result of demonic influence. This is nothing to be afraid of; however, it is reality. And unless we are aware of this, the enemy can easily manipulate us through dreams and use them to cause fear, anxiety, division, suspicion, accusation, and the like.

For instance, the devil may give you a dream that would divide you from other people. Such destructive dreams will often involve some of the most important people in your life. I've had dreams where the key people in my life were betraying me, and suspicion arose in my heart because of the dream I had about that person. I literally woke up feeling suspicious of the person—either consciously or subconsciously. Just as the Holy Spirit can speak to us, so can the enemy, who prowls around like a ravenous lion attempting to destroy us by telling us lies.

Over time I became better at discerning dreams where the enemy was wanting to sow division between me and the most important people in my life. I had to be aware that just because I had a dream about a certain person, it didn't necessarily mean the dream was from the Lord.

As you press in to the Lord and grow in your ability to dream His dreams and flow more effectively in the supernatural, you will also grow in your ability to discern which dreams are from your natural mind, which dreams are from the enemy, and which dreams are from the Lord.

DREAMS ARE A MYSTERY

At their core, dreams are a mystery. We go about our lives doing our daily activities. And then we lay our heads on our pillows at night and close our eyes, and who knows where we end up going. We wake up the next morning having experienced something unexpected or amazing in our dreams and wondering, "Why did I dream that? Why did I travel on that journey through my dream, and how could that have been created while I was sleeping?"

You know, scientists can measure certain things in test tubes and with instruments, but can anybody truly explain dreams? Dream experts can tell us why and when we dream, but they can't tell us where dreams come from. Dreams are beyond the realm of the natural world. People appear in our dreams whom we've never met, and they have personalities. I've even heard heavenly music in my dreams at night, music that is more beautiful than anything I have ever heard in this world.

Dreams are vital because when we dream, it's actually as if we are living those experiences. We feel them, and they leave an imprint on us. Have you ever woken up after a vivid dream and wondered why you dreamed what you did? Perhaps it had no connection to anything you read or saw on television. But it was just so *real*, and the characters in the dream had such distinct personalities that you wondered, "Where in the world did *that* come from?"

When we're awake, we're typically very fixed on our material surroundings. If we're at work, for example, we're engaged with the task at hand. If we're driving an automobile, we're focused on the cars in front of us, the stop signs, the ever-changing signals, and so on. But when we're dreaming, our souls are loose from the material world, and they're in a state that is more open to hearing from God. It's as if the soul is hovering between the spiritual and natural worlds. As we sleep, then, we are actually in a great position to receive revelation that we might otherwise miss when we are awake.

When we sleep, we disconnect from the distractions of the material world—all our worries, anxieties, and preoccupations—and tune in to a state where we can more readily hear and receive what God wants to communicate to us.

THE LANGUAGE OF DREAMS

What's interesting is that the language of prophetic dreams is similar to the type of language Jesus used when He spoke to His disciples in parables. In other words, frequently when we receive a dream that's from the Lord, the message God communicates may not be clear or straightforward.

Rather than the meaning or interpretation being right in front of our face, the message may come to us in symbolic form. We see a clear example of this in the story of Joseph in Genesis 37. God gave Joseph a series of dreams where he saw sheaves of grain and then the sun, moon, and stars bowing down before him (vv. 5–7, 9). But Joseph didn't understand the meaning of his dreams until years later when he, through a series of dramatic circumstances, had been promoted to second-in-command in the land of Egypt. And when there was a famine in Canaan, where Joseph's family was living, they came to him in Egypt to buy grain and literally bowed before him there. Then Joseph understood that his dreams about the sheaves, sun, moon, and stars bowing down to him had to come to pass. God didn't make His message clear to Joseph and just show him that eventually his family would bow down to him. Instead He veiled the meaning with mysterious symbols like sheaves of grain and the sun, moon, and stars.

Consider that when we examine the parables of Jesus, we see that He commonly used symbols to communicate revelations to His followers. Why did Jesus teach this way? I believe one reason is so His followers would not just listen to His words but concentrate and hear the deeper meaning. Jesus was attempting to reach people at a spiritual level—to break through the noise and distractions of the material world to get to the heart of the matter and get to the spiritual truths of His teachings.

When we know God has spoken something to us in our dreams, but we're not quite sure what He's saying, we have to seek Him for understanding. And because the dream drives us to seek Him, our relationship with the Lord is strengthened. God speaks in mysteries because He wants to involve us in the discovery.

It reminds me of a father and child working together on a jigsaw puzzle. Alone, the child might never figure out the puzzle. But when the father engages with the child, the child is suddenly able to make sense of the puzzle, and intimacy is created as father and child work together. On the other hand, if the father puts all the pieces together by himself, the child is a mere bystander—there is no engagement. This is one of the best ways to know that a dream is neither a natural one nor something from the enemy: God engages with us in the process of discovery. As we look to and depend on HaShem for the understanding of our dreams, intimacy with Him through Messiah Jesus is developed.

SEEK AND YOU WILL FIND

Jesus said, "Seek, and ye shall find" (Matt. 7:7, KJV). We need to seek God's face for both the source and meanings of our dreams.

As we draw closer to Him in this process, we will come to more accurately hear His voice and understand what He is trying to say to us. Again, notice that this is the same principle Yeshua used when He spoke in parables. Consider this passage from the Book of Mark:

> And He said, "How shall we picture the kingdom of God, or by what parable shall we present it? It is like a mustard seed, which, when sown upon the soil, though it is smaller than all the seeds that are upon the soil, yet when it is sown, it grows up and becomes larger than all the garden plants and forms large branches; so that the birds of the air can nest under its shade."
> —MARK 4:30–32

Now notice what the next verse says:

> With many such parables He was speaking the word to them, so far as they were able to hear it; and He

did not speak to them without a parable; but He was explaining everything privately to His own disciples.

—Mark 4:33

After Yeshua told the parable about the sower and the seed (Luke 8), we read:

His disciples began questioning Him as to what this parable meant. And He said, "To you it has been granted to know the mysteries of the kingdom of God."

—Luke 8:9–10

After the disciples asked for the parable's interpretation, Yeshua gave it to them. In other words, Yeshua was relying heavily on parables because He was both revealing and concealing truth at the same time. He was revealing truth in a limited way. Why? Because in order for the disciples to fully understand the truth that He was revealing, they had to come to Him and inquire, "What did You mean?" They had to press in; they had to seek Him.

For example, when we hear the parable about the sower and the seed, we may instantly know the interpretation. But that's because the disciples first inquired as to the interpretation, and then the true meaning was recorded in Scripture. This is true of many of the parables written in the Gospels: Jesus shared the parable and then followed it with the interpretation so the disciples would understand.

But when the disciples first heard the parable about the mustard seed, or about the seeds being sown, they didn't know the interpretations. The Scriptures say they had to go to ask Jesus privately, and then Yeshua explained it to them. Obviously, if Yeshua wanted everyone to know the point of the parables, He would have spoken in clearer language. He wasn't trying to be coy or cunning—He had a purpose for His use of symbolism.

In Judaism there is a concept called *devekut*. It means "clinging on to God" and points to the fact that one of the primary elements of walking with God is to *cling* to Him.[1] God wants you and me to constantly cling to Him or be brought close by depending on Him and looking to Him for the interpretation of our dreams, which again is one reason He often uses symbolic imagery and language when He speaks to us through dreams. God's love draws us toward Him, and He uses the symbolism and mystery of parables and dreams to engage us and make us active participants with Him. As we seek the Lord, we will find Him.

HEARING GOD AUDIBLY IN DREAMS

Most of the time God speaks to me through imagery— simple pictures of scenes, people, and so forth that communicate a message. But there are times when the Lord will speak to us audibly in our dreams at night. Consider, for example, what happened with Solomon.

> In Gibeon the LORD appeared to Solomon in a dream at night; and God said, "Ask what you wish Me to give you."
>
> —1 KINGS 3:5

Solomon literally heard the voice of God say to him, "Ask what you wish Me to give you." This is not a means of prophetic communication relegated only to Bible times. Sometimes God will literally speak to us in an audible voice. I've had this happen on several occasions.

I remember having a spiritual encounter with the Lord one night about fifteen years ago. It was like there was a river of fire rolling into me, then back to God, into me, and back to God—like a circling river of fire. Then the Holy Spirit spoke audibly to me and said, "Seize My Word and don't let anything else in." There's nothing in the world that could ever make me doubt that I heard the voice of Father God that night. I've grieved over the message He spoke because sometimes I struggle to fully comprehend and obey that word. For example, sometimes I still allow thoughts of worry or fear into my life. And when that happens, I have to consciously lift my soul back up to HaShem, asking Him for help to come into alignment with His Spirit, His truth, and His Word and not let the darkness in. I pray even to this day: "Lord, help me to seize Your Word and not let anything else in."

As I began to pray and seek the Lord, He began to help me understand what He was saying to me. God wanted me to seize the portion of His Word that He was highlighting to me at that particular season in my life and not let anything else in. Whether it's the written Word of God or something the Father has spoken to me through a dream or prophetic word, I am to seize His Word and not let anything else in.

The enemy is always out there trying to give us a false perception of reality. But God was saying to me—and I believe to you also—"Don't let the voice of darkness in. Don't let the enemy's perception of reality invade your consciousness, but seize My Word and don't let anything else in." Beloved, God speaks to us through our dreams—not just to some of us, but to all of us. Oftentimes He speaks using pictures, symbols, and figurative language, and sometimes He speaks audibly.

To disregard our dreams is to disregard God.

How to Know If a Dream Is From God

I want to close this chapter by providing some keys to help you know whether or not a dream is from God. As you seek to discern whether a dream is from God, consider the following questions.

1. **Does the dream line up with God's Word?**
   If you're not sure whether a dream lines up with the teachings of Scripture, don't accept it right away as a prophetic dream. For example, many have gotten divorced and remarried because they "dreamed" about being in a relationship with someone else. They were convinced their dream was from God, and it was His will for them to divorce and remarry the person in their dream. But no matter how good that dream may have felt, how real it seemed, or how much they may have believed it came from God's Spirit, the Word of God says, "I hate divorce" (Mal. 2:16). The dream must be rejected because it directly contradicts God's Word. This example may seem basic or simple, but unfortunately, this has happened many times. If you're not sure what the Scriptures may have to say about your dream, seek counsel from a mature brother or sister who is well-versed in God's Word.

2. **Does the dream resonate with your spirit?** Though the Bible is our standard for measuring the content of our dreams, pray for the Holy Spirit to validate the source. Ask God, "Where did this dream come from? Was this from You? Please show me its origin."

3. **Have you received confirmation of the dream?** As I have shared, many times when I did not understand a dream's meaning, God later confirmed it and gave me understanding through an event or circumstance in my life. Sometimes God will instantly confirm a dream, and sometimes it may take years.

Before you go to sleep at night, pray that your dreams will be "authored" by the Spirit of God. Also, ask God to protect your mind and soul as you sleep, and to guard you from demonic dreams. I have found that when I pray this before I fall asleep, I am better able to ascertain whether or not a dream I have is from God.

TYPES OF DREAMS

W E CAN'T PREDICT how or when God will speak to us. His ways are above our ways, and His thoughts are above our thoughts. Sometimes He'll speak to us about something we are going through in our current season. Other times He will speak to us about something that is yet to come so we will be prepared when it manifests. Sometimes God will reveal Himself through a dream to build confidence in us; at other times He will bring a word of warning. Sometimes it's a word of strategy or direction. God will even use dreams to give us insight into some-body else's life so we can know how to minister to them.

The point is that God uses dreams in a multitude of ways. In this chapter I share several of the ways the Lord has directed my life through dreams. I am not doing this to draw attention to myself, but rather to show you how real and practical God's employment of dreams in your life can be.

Let's begin by examining how God can use dreams to help us understand our calling or destiny. Sometimes the Lord will give us a dream about our future so that when the future arrives—when the future becomes now—we'll know what to do.

DREAMS THAT REVEAL THE FUTURE

More than thirty years ago, before I got married, the Lord gave me such a dream, and it would be many years before I would see the dream realized. In this particular dream I was standing in the attic of a home. It was a very simple room, rectangular in shape, and it appeared to be about thirty feet long and twelve feet wide. There were two windows—one on each side—and it was dark. There were other people in the attic with me, and we were standing against the back wall.

Suddenly, from one of the two windows came a bright stream of light that contained all the colors of the rainbow. It was flowing like a river through the window and was unlike anything I'd ever seen. The best way I can describe it is to say it was about a foot and a half high and looked like living, multidimensional crepe paper. It was a beautiful spirit of flowing life containing all the colors of the rainbow.

I stepped away from the back wall and moved toward the window where the rainbow light was flowing in. When I reached the window, I stuck my head outside, and everywhere I looked there was brilliant color. It was an eternity of color. In the dream I opened my arms and said, "Come and live inside me!" And I immediately heard the word *eternity* deep down in my soul.

Then the dream instantly shifted, and I found myself looking out the other window, the one on the other side of the room. There was chaos—all kinds of random stuff was just floating across the window.

Then *bam*! The scene shifted again. In the third and final phase of the dream, I was walking down a street, feeling completely at peace. As I was walking, I came upon the scene of a car accident. I approached a wrecked car and saw an African man in the vehicle who was clearly injured.

As I approached him, I could see that he was badly burned from the accident. And without thinking, I simply and calmly held my hand out toward him. As my hand was extended toward him, the rainbow colors that I had asked to come live inside me (in the first part of the dream) came flowing out of my fingertips and over the African man's body. I stood there amazed as the man was healed of his injuries. Then the dream was over.

That dream had a very powerful effect on me and my ministry. When I had the dream, I knew it was from God and that He was calling me into a healing ministry that would involve the African people. I had never been to Africa, so at first I thought the dream pertained to African Americans.

The years passed, and although I had intentionally tried to reach African Americans through television, I did not feel that my dream had fully come to pass. Then about ten years ago I received a call from someone in Haiti who asked me to come and minister there. I accepted the invitation, and when I preached in Haiti, literally thousands of people ran forward to accept Jesus as their Messiah. Even though I was in a Caribbean nation, I realized that most Haitian people have African roots, their ancestors having originally been brought there as slaves.

From there, I saw God begin to open doors for me to travel in Africa. And over a period of several years I was focused on doing ministry in a particular nation on the African continent. We were seeing tremendous fruit, with the crowds in the tens of thousands at our evening outreaches. And I knew the dream I'd had roughly thirty years earlier, bringing healing to Africans, had come to pass.

God gave me a dream about ministering to Africans approximately thirty years before the fulfillment manifested. But God also used a dream to prepare me for a future event that was only a few days away.

During one particular trip to Africa, where I was to conduct an outreach, we were greeted by large crowds of people lining the streets, awaiting our arrival. I'm talking about thousands and thousands of people standing along the route they knew we would be traveling as we entered their city. There was also a military band welcoming us. It was surreal.

I remember saying to myself, "If the number of people who turned out to greet us is anywhere representative of the number of people who will come to the crusade, this will be our biggest outreach yet in this nation." After the reception I had dinner, checked into my hotel, and went to sleep, because the first of our nightly evangelism outreaches was to be held the next day.

Early in the morning, just before I woke up, I had a dream. In it I saw a river, and as I looked down the river, I saw a huge houseboat that had run aground in shallow water. The water level had dropped so much that the water could no longer support the weight of the boat, and it wasn't going anywhere. Somehow in the dream I knew the houseboat belonged to me.

I looked downriver to see if there was a way through—if I could free the boat from the shallows. But when I looked downstream, I could see the mist and hear the roar of a large waterfall. As I looked upstream, I could see huge boulders strewn across the river. I wondered how the boat could have gotten there in the first place, past all those boulders.

Then the dream ended, and I woke up. Shortly after that my prayer minister came to my door to talk and pray about the day's events. I said, "I just had this dream. I think God spoke to me, and somehow it has to do with our outreach here." After I told my prayer minister the dream, he began to pray about it. And because the dream was not positive (in the sense that the boat was grounded), he began to rebuke the dream and prophesy that we would have great meetings.

Well, we went to the first meeting, and only about five thousand people turned out. By American standards that may sound like a lot, but we were used to seeing between thirty thousand and fifty-five thousand people each night. The next night was the same thing—about five thousand. I said, "Well, maybe on Saturday the crowd will really blow up. They will turn out on the weekend." On Saturday, however, the crowd was about the same size.

On Sunday I was on my way to the crusade when the Holy Spirit spoke to me. He said, "Remember that dream I showed you with the boat run aground in the river? The boat that was grounded is your ministry—it has gone as far as it can go in this nation. Your ministry will not go any further here right now just like the boat in the dream could not go farther down the river. Now I'm opening up a door for you in another country." Sure enough, almost immediately God opened up doors for us in another country where we saw tremendous attendance and fruit.

It's powerful how the Lord uses dreams to speak to us. My well-intentioned prayer minister had rebuked the dream, thinking it was not from God. At the time I really wasn't sure either. But then God was faithful to confirm the dream through the relatively small size of the crowds, and then through my intuition, and then by sending us to a new nation almost immediately where we had great success in the Lord. This is a perfect example of how God will confirm that a dream is indeed from Him rather than simply a natural dream or one that comes from the enemy.

I have been able to make many critical decisions with confidence because the Lord showed me what to do in advance through a dream. Perhaps you can relate to what I am talking about. Maybe the Lord showed you something about your destiny well before it became a reality in your life. As with me, the reason He showed you beforehand was so when your destiny came, you'd be able to recognize it and walk through that door with assurance. When I saw the dream I just described come to pass (by observing the small crowds that were not growing), I was able to immediately turn my attention to another nation rather than continuing to labor in a place where we were no longer seeing fruit. Just as the boat in my dream could go no farther down the river, we weren't able to go further in that nation in that season. Our mission was complete.

God wants to counsel you about your future, beloved. He used two very specific dreams, given twenty-five years apart, to open the door for me to minister in Africa and then to guide me when it was time to shift my focus from one African nation to another.

His timing is not our timing, and for God "one day is like a thousand years, and a thousand years like one day" (2 Pet. 3:8). The seed of that healing ministry to Africa had been planted twenty-five years before it came to pass. And though it took a quarter century, when the opportunity arose to minister to the peoples of Africa, I knew it was God.

DREAMS THAT PROVIDE DIRECTION

As we have seen in previous chapters, God also uses dreams to give us specific words of direction for our life.

We see this in the Book of Matthew when God spoke to Joseph about how to protect the baby Jesus:

> But when Herod died, behold, an angel of the Lord appeared in a dream to Joseph in Egypt, and said, "Get up, take the Child and His mother, and go into the land of Israel; for those who sought the Child's life are dead."
>
> —MATTHEW 2:19–20

Previously, God had told Joseph in a dream to take Yeshua into Egypt to protect Him after Herod issued an edict to kill every male child in Bethlehem under the age of two. Then in a subsequent dream (in the passage we just read) He told Joseph to take Yeshua back to Israel. God gave Joseph personalized direction and strategy. God did not reveal the timing and strategy to Joseph through the Scriptures (the Torah at that time). Instead He sent an angel to speak directly to Joseph and give him very specific details about where and when to go. That is how Joseph knew exactly how to take care of the baby Jesus.

Let me give you another example of a directional dream. Years ago I dreamed I was in a room that was about twenty feet long and eight feet wide. There was a couch against one wall, and sitting on the couch were a middle-aged man and woman. The woman was sitting in the middle, and I was seated next to her with my head leaning on her shoulder.

The scene felt like the passage in Psalms where David says that he had stilled his soul by resting against his mother:

> Surely I have composed and quieted my soul; like
> a weaned child rests against his mother, my soul is
> like a weaned child within me.
>
> —Psalm 131:2

In the dream I was leaning my head on this woman's shoulder, and I felt a deep sense of security. This symbolized the security a child has in his relationship with his mama. And as I was resting in this deep place of security, I said to the man, "What do you think of Jesus?"

Then immediately the dream shifted. I found myself in a very similar room, and I was sitting on the couch once again. This time there was a young woman, about twenty-two years of age, standing in the center of the room. I said the same thing to this young woman: "What do you think of Jesus?" And she said, "Well, I know He said a lot to the world and to the church, but He never said anything to me, like about being boyfriend, girlfriend." Then suddenly the dream was over.

I was very struck by how strange the young woman's language was. It was not anything I would have thought someone would say, nor was it language I would use. That is when I began to suspect that God had spoken to me. In other words, the unusual details and clarity of the dream helped me realize that it was a prophetic dream.

Immediately I got out of bed, thought and prayed about the dream, and wrote it down. I felt very strongly the dream was from HaShem but had to seek in the Spirit for its meaning. As I sought the Lord for the interpretation, here is what I believe I discerned.

The first thing I perceived from that two-phased dream was a specific witnessing question to use. I actually train people how to share the gospel and encourage them to use that exact question as a lead-in: What do you think of Jesus?

Notice that the question wasn't "What do you think *about* Jesus?" If you ask someone what they think *about* Jesus, the person might give you an intellectual "head" answer or something he or she read in a history book. But if you say "What do you think *of* Jesus?" you've asked a more personal, open-ended question. And the person will be more likely to share with you what he or she really believes.

From that same dream I received two other revelations. The first had to do with the first phase of the dream when I was leaning my head on the woman's shoulder. To be clear, there was nothing sexual about the gesture; I never even saw the woman's face. As I said, it was just a strong picture of security—like the way a child feels in the safety of his or her mother.

It was from that place of security that I was able to begin to witness to the man by asking, "What do you think of Jesus?" I believe the Lord was saying to me that many men do not share their faith, because they're insecure. They're afraid they won't be looked at as macho if they tell another man about Jesus. The Lord was sharing with me, "I want you to challenge men to be secure and share their faith with other men."

Then I began to inquire about the second phase of the dream, involving the young woman. The Lord showed me that when a lot of people think about Jesus, they just think about the fact that "God so loved the world." Remember what the young woman said to me in the dream: "Well, I know He said a lot to the world and to the church, but He never said anything to me, like about being boyfriend, girlfriend." The Lord was saying to me, "When you share

My love with people, they need to understand that I love them individually, personally, and specifically." This young woman only knew the "church Jesus." She didn't know Him as someone who wanted to be in an intimate relationship with her and who could fulfill her deepest longing for connection. So the Lord was showing me in the dream, "When you share My love with people, they need to hear how much I uniquely cherish them. They need to understand that I have called them to the marriage supper of the Lamb." (See Revelation 19:9.)

I learned from that dream that when I share the love of Jesus with people, they need to understand that it's not just a message for the world—it's a message for them individually, specifically, and personally.

DREAMS THAT ENCOURAGE

Sometimes we can receive comfort and encouragement from God through our dreams in a way that far surpasses the comfort that any human being could ever give us. This is especially true when we're going through hard times in our lives.

Let's take a look at a scriptural example of this in Genesis 28. In this passage Jacob is fleeing for his life after stealing the birthright of his older brother, Esau, who is out to kill him. If you recall, Jacob had tricked his father, Isaac, into giving him Esau's birthright. Jacob ran away from the only home he had ever known, and as night fell, he found himself in a foreign land all alone. But he had a dream that night. We read:

> He had a dream, and behold, a ladder was set on the
> earth with its top reaching to heaven; and behold,
> the angels of God were ascending and descending

on it. And behold, the Lord stood above it and said, "I am the Lord, the God of your father Abraham and the God of Isaac; the land on which you lie, I will give it to you and to your descendants. Your descendants will also be like the dust of the earth, and you will spread out to the west and to the east and to the north and to the south; and in you and in your descendants shall all the families of the earth be blessed. Behold, I am with you and will keep you wherever you go, and will bring you back to this land; for I will not leave you until I have done what I have promised you." Then Jacob awoke from his sleep and said, "Surely the Lord is in this place, and I did not know it."

—Genesis 28:11–16

I want to provide a bit of context for what happened to Jacob when he fled Beersheba, his homeland. It wasn't like today where you can move across the country with relative ease. Today cross-country moves are fairly common, and it's possible to acclimate to a new area relatively quickly.

Compare that to what life was like in the ancient biblical world, when families tended to stay in one place. And traveling, of course, was by foot or camel, for the most part. Your whole family lived in one place, and you'd never known anything outside that location. Imagine growing up in that kind of culture and then having to leave that geographical area to go someplace that's completely unfamiliar.

That was the case with Jacob—but it was even worse, because he was also facing possible death if his brother, Esau, were to find him. And in that state he went to sleep one night with a rock as a pillow.

As Jacob was sleeping, he had a remarkable dream where he saw angels ascending and descending an enormous ladder reaching to heaven. And then God told him that his descendants would be "like the dust of the earth" and that He was going to give Jacob the land upon which he was lying. Talk about a powerful, dramatic dream!

Jacob woke up and as a result of the dream said, "Surely the LORD is in this place; and I knew it not" (v. 16, KJV). Jacob realized that God was with him right where he was, and it took away his fear. He also discovered that God's favor was on him and his future descendants. This all happened because of a dream he received in the night!

Years ago I was going through a season of deep pain. In the midst of this difficult season I had a dream one night in which I literally heard an angel speak to me. I knew it was an angel rather than the Holy Spirit. The angel said, "You are on the right path." Just six words—but they brought deep assurance to me during a very hard time. Even though I was going through a deep time of hurt and confusion, that night I knew I was walking in God's love, His favor was on me, and I was on the right path—all because an angel spoke to me in my dream.

Now, you may be thinking, "How can you be sure it was an angel?" All I can tell you is that when you encounter the Lord, or when you encounter an angel, there is no question as to what's going on. The Bible says that in the day of God's power, man is made willing (Ps. 110:3). You will just know.

DREAMS THAT WARN

In addition to giving me direction, the Lord has warned me in dreams at night of things that could happen if I didn't heed the counsel. There are many examples of this in Scripture. For example, in Matthew 2, the same chapter in which God warned Joseph to take the baby Jesus and Mary to Egypt, He also warned the wise men after they had visited the newly born Messiah:

> And having been warned by God in a dream not to return to Herod, the magi left for their own country by another way.
>
> —MATTHEW 2:12

At this point in Scripture, Yeshua had been born, and the magi had come from far away to pay their respects and give gifts to the newborn Messiah. Now it was time to go home, and they were unaware of an unseen danger. So the Lord rerouted them. How did the wise men gain God's strategy for their journey home? Through their dreams.

Heeding God's warnings can prevent you from making all kinds of wrong choices—from getting involved in the wrong relationships to making the wrong purchases. God can help you to stay on track if you'll pay attention, particularly to the warnings He gives you at night. As Job's friend Elihu said, the Lord can save your soul from the pit if you'll listen to His warnings to you through your dreams at night. (See Job 33.)

I remember some years ago that Cynthia and I were thinking of purchasing a home in a community that was some distance from where we had been living. We went and looked at this home, and there were some advantages to it, and the price was right. So we signed a contract. That night I went back over to the home I had under contract, and I saw a bench outside. So I sat down there, and

I prayed, "Lord, do You want me to purchase this home?" Then after praying for a little while, I left.

That same night I had a dream where I saw myself in a stockade (an enclosure for military prisoners) on the property I was in contract to purchase. The image of the stockade in the dream was so scary that I knew if I bought that house, I'd feel trapped. Believe me, I called that realtor first thing in the morning and cancelled the contract. The Lord saved me from making a decision that could have gravely impacted my life by warning me in a dream.

SOME DREAMS ARE BEYOND CATEGORY

Sometimes our Father speaks to us simply as a result of our being in relationship with Him. Because He loves us, He communicates with us. I mentioned in a previous chapter that God spoke audibly to Solomon in a dream. Here I want us to look at the full exchange:

> In that night God appeared to Solomon and said to him, "Ask what I shall give you." Solomon said to God, "You have dealt with my father David with great lovingkindness, and have made me king in his place. Now, O LORD God, Your promise to my father David is fulfilled, for You have made me king over a people as numerous as the dust of the earth. Give me now wisdom and knowledge, that I may go out and come in before this people, for who can rule this great people of Yours?" God said to Solomon, "Because you had this in mind, and did not ask for riches, wealth or honor, or the life of those who hate you, nor have you even asked for long life, but you have asked for yourself wisdom and knowledge that you may rule My people over

whom I have made you king, wisdom and knowledge have been granted to you. And I will give you
riches and wealth and honor, such as none of the
kings who were before you has possessed nor those
who will come after you."

—2 Chronicles 1:7–12

In this dream God was simply relating to Solomon as His son. It reflected the intimacy of their relationship.

I have experienced similar dreams. Some years back I had a dream in which I was walking with a friend to a tryout for a big baseball tournament. My friend was a tremendous athlete, so in the dream I just assumed I was there to support him. So we walked to this baseball tryout and approached the coach running it.

Unexpectedly, the coach looked at me. And I'm thinking, "Why is he looking at me? My friend's the athlete." I was kind of a one-dimensional athlete. I could wrestle—that was it. But the coach said to me in the dream, "Everything that's happened in your life up to this point is water under the bridge. But I'm going to be watching you from this point forward to determine whether I'm going to put you in the major leagues."

And then the dream was over. So it was kind of an astonishing dream because, again, my friend was the gifted athlete, not me! Why would the coach say he was going to be watching me to see if I was good enough for the majors?

I keep a dream journal, which I encourage you to do too (more on that later in the book), and I write down the dreams I think are from God. So I wrote down this dream, even though I didn't know the interpretation, and I prayed about it.

Almost a year later I was going through my dream journal on New Year's Day. This is something I always do on the first of the year to see how God has spoken to me the previous year. As I was going through the dream journal, I saw the major league dream, which I'd forgotten about. As I was reading, I immediately felt defeated because I knew how selfish and self-centered I can be. Thoughts of defeat filled my mind as I reread the entry.

I knew the coach in the dream was a symbol of the Lord, and when I reviewed my dream journal, I didn't think I had a chance in the world of having "made the cut" for God to promote me to the majors. (The majors for me would have been God taking me to the next level in ministry and giving me a major platform to reach the world for Him.)

In my desperation I opened my Bible and said to the Lord, "If my finger lands on a Q, I know You are telling me I made it to the majors. And if it lands on an X, I will know that You are not." Please understand, I am not recommending this method, and God certainly doesn't have to speak this way. I am just being authentic with you. I know this is not a foolproof approach—but I felt desperate!

I randomly threw open my Bible and asked the Lord to take me to either a Q or an X. I closed my eyes and stabbed my finger on a random page. As I opened my eyes, I saw neither a Q nor an X.

My finger had landed on the word *major.*

I was blown away. I mean, I didn't even realize the word *major* was in the Bible.

I typically use the New American Standard Version (NASB), so I went to Bible Gateway and typed in the word *major.* How many times is the word *major* in the Bible? The website showed four results, so I looked up the four references. Much to my astonishment, in three of the four references the word *major* wasn't used, but the word *majority* (which contains the word *major*). In other words, the word *major* is used once in the NASB. Out of the more than 750,000 words in that translation of the Bible, my finger landed on the one time the word *major* is used.

I was blown away by what God showed me, because I simply did not feel I deserved to be used in a "major league" way by Him! But you know, God is so much more tender toward you and me than we realize. He's so much softer than we understand. David said of the Lord, "Your gentleness has made me great" (Ps. 18:35, NKJV).

After that dream we were given a prime-time spot on the largest Christian television network in the world. And we saw one of our African outreaches reach an estimated one hundred thousand in attendance. When those two things happened, I thought, "Wow, Lord. You really did bring me into the major league."

Beloved, God uses dreams to meet you at the point of your need. He may use a dream to heal past wounds of trauma. Or He may speak to you about your present, thus helping you make vital decisions for your life and family. And because He is the God of the future, He may give you dreams of direction or warning to help you navigate things that are yet to come. But no matter what kind of dream He gives, you will be blessed by following God's leading through your dreams.

CHAPTER 5

RECEIVING REVELATION FROM YOUR DREAMS

W E'VE ESTABLISHED THE fact that God uses dreams as a consistent, common tool in both the Old and New Testaments. We have also talked about how since Pentecost, God has provided the Holy Spirit for us to experience and hear His voice. As we develop "ears to hear" God in our dreams, we will be able to more easily determine whether our dreams are from our natural mind, the enemy, or the Lord.

When we know a dream is from the Lord, we need to take it very seriously by earnestly seeking the meaning and interpretation of the dream. Dreams are weighty because dreams carry the voice of God. This means that *to disregard your dreams is to disregard God's voice*. I know that is a strong statement. But if God considers dreams to be important, so should we, and the value we place on our dreams will be evident in how we handle them.

Through the years I have often seen people struggle to understand their dreams because of how cryptic they can be. Because dreams often come to us in symbolic language, we have to learn how to interpret them. That is my goal in this chapter—to equip you to consistently and accurately receive the interpretation of the dreams God gives you.

UNDERSTANDING YOUR DREAMS

Oftentimes we miss the boat, not in recognizing if a dream is from the Lord but in our interpretation of it and response to it. In other words, we are ascertaining correctly that we had a God dream, but things may sometimes break down in our interpretation and application of it.

This has happened to me. Many times when the Lord gave me dreams, my initial thought of what the dream meant wasn't correct. It was only through persevering in prayer for the interpretation that the Holy Spirit brought the correct meaning into focus.

Let me give you a clear example of this. Approximately ten years ago I had a very vivid dream while I was pastoring a Messianic congregation. In the dream, I was preaching; then suddenly, in the middle of my message, the congregation stood up, put their hands over their hearts, and in unison started saying, "I pledge allegiance to the flag of the United States of America..." The congregation's voice literally drowned out my preaching. I was so humiliated and overwhelmed in the dream as this was happening that I walked out of the sanctuary and went into the restroom in our congregational building.

In the restroom I cried out to my Father God about this, and He said to me, "Go back in and finish your message." So I went back to the sanctuary, and when I walked in, one of the congregants shouted at me, "They don't want to listen to you anymore!" In obedience I pressed on to finish my message, but it was very, very difficult. And then the dream ended.

This dream really unsettled me, and immediately I began to cry out to Father for the interpretation. I began to think, "What am I doing wrong that the congregation would stand up in the middle of the message and drown me out while I am preaching?" So I prayed, "Abba, Lord, what am I doing wrong? Where am I failing as a leader? What weakness or insecurity is the congregation seeing in me that they would rebel like this?" I went on praying like this, looking to the Lord for the interpretation, for several days.

After praying for a few days, I was in a hotel room one night getting ready to preach at a church the next morning. I was still calling out to HaShem about this dream, asking Him where I was failing as a leader. Then suddenly, in a burst of divine revelation, God breathed into me the interpretation. I didn't hear an audible voice, but I absolutely knew in my spirit that God had revealed to me the interpretation of the dream. And here's what it was.

He said: "I wasn't showing you that you were a weak leader. I was showing you that the people's allegiance is not to Me but to the pursuit of the American dream. In their pursuit of the American dream [which was evidenced by them saying the Pledge of Allegiance] they are blocking out My Word from their life. Their desire for the things of the world is drowning out their desire for Me in their life."

Again, this experience shows that when the Lord gives us a dream, our initial belief about what it means may not be correct. That is why we need to keep on praying until we're really settled and have a clear understanding of its meaning and feel God's confirmation of it. The Lord was speaking powerfully to me through that dream, and if I hadn't continued to press in to Him for understanding, I would have missed the dream's true meaning.

THE SOURCE OF REVELATION

The most important thing to realize as you seek to understand your dreams is this: the same One who gave you the dream—HaShem, Father God—will also give you its meaning as you look to Him prayerfully and consistently for the interpretation. We see an example of this in Daniel 2. King Nebuchadnezzar had a dream and knew it was from the Lord, but he didn't know the meaning.

> Then Arioch hurriedly brought Daniel into the king's presence and spoke to him as follows: "I have found a man among the exiles from Judah who can make the interpretation known to the king!" The king said to Daniel, whose name was Belteshazzar, "Are you able to make known to me the dream which I have seen and its interpretation?" Daniel answered before the king and said, "As for the mystery about which the king has inquired, neither wise men, conjurers, magicians nor diviners are able to declare it to the king. However, there is a God in heaven who reveals mysteries, and He has made known to King Nebuchadnezzar what will take place in the latter days. This was your dream and the visions in your mind while on your bed."
>
> —DANIEL 2:25–28

Daniel went on to interpret the king's dream, but as you can see, he first made it clear who gave him the revelation. Daniel said in essence, "It's not in me to know the interpretation, but God will reveal the mystery to you." This is the most important thing to understand as you seek understanding of your dreams—the interpretation comes from the Lord.

When you have a dream, sometimes it's good to talk it over with people, especially a spouse or a very close loved one, someone who has spiritual discernment. Sometimes as you talk through the dream with someone, the interpretation will come into focus. But ultimately, the One who is going to give you the interpretation of the dream is the same One who gave you the dream in the first place. As you seek God in prayer for the interpretation, the revelation will come.

FIVE STEPS TO HEARING FROM GOD THROUGH YOUR DREAMS

Perhaps you are thinking, "Rabbi, this is wonderful information, and I am excited to hear more from God in my dreams. But where do I start? It all feels a bit overwhelming!" I can understand if you are wondering how to begin. So, to bring this message down to a very practical level, I want to share a few simple things you can do to better hear—and remember—the dreams God gives you.

We have already talked about some of these steps, but they are so important that they bear repeating. These also are tools you can use as you begin to record your dreams in the "Your Dream Journal" section of this book, which immediately follows this chapter.

Before you get out of bed each morning, do the following:

1. Spend time alone with God in the silence, listening for His voice.

When you first wake up, allow yourself to be alone with Father God. Turn off the television and refrain from texting. Just be still with Him, perhaps with gentle worship music playing. Don't talk to anyone, not your spouse, children, roommate—not anybody. As you make a practice of tuning in to the Father first thing each day, He will keep your heart and soul quieted and open to hear His voice.

2. Ask God if He spoke to you in your dreams.

After silencing your spirit and tuning in to God, ask, "Father, did I dream anything last night? Did You speak to me in my dreams?" Fight the temptation to get busy or start thinking about what you need to accomplish that day. If you do that, you'll forget any dreams you had the night before. Even before your feet hit the floor, and while you are still waking up from the night before, ask God if He visited you in a dream. Remember what Elihu said in Job 33:14–16: "Indeed God speaks once, or twice, yet no one notices it. In a dream, a vision of the night, when sound sleep falls on men, while they slumber in their beds, then He opens the ears of men, and seals their instruction."

3. Start your day slowly instead of rushing into your daily routine.

Give yourself time to get out of bed slowly. Don't rush around like a chicken with its head cut off, hurrying to work, school, or wherever you're going. Wake up early enough to give yourself time to hear from God about the dreams of the previous night while they are still fresh in your mind. I recommend spending at least thirty minutes alone with the Lord.

4. Have your dream journal ready and write down any dreams you remember.

If you believe God may have spoken to you in a dream, talk to Him about it—don't discuss the dream with other people first. Then write down what you remember about the dream and anything the Lord brings to mind. As you begin writing, the details will come. You will sometimes begin to remember more as you start writing. Don't censor yourself. Write everything that comes to mind. You may be surprised how significant the smallest details can be.

As you write down your dream, record as many details as you can recall, but don't mix your interpretation in at this point. Just write down the dream exactly as it happened.

You may think writing down your dreams is unnecessary, but I have found that if God speaks to me in a dream and I don't take time to write it down and talk to the Lord about it, I'll forget about it, and the dream will have little impact. But when I make time to honor God's word to me by writing down my dreams, the dreams are transferred from my short-term memory to my long-term memory. And I am able to go back and review the dreams a month, a year, or even a decade later.

I know it takes work to get up a little bit earlier to spend time with the Lord and implement my recommendations, especially if you are on a tight schedule. But as we discussed at the beginning of this chapter, if you value your relationship with God, you will value the messages He gives you through your dreams.

5. Seek in the Spirit for the interpretation.

After you have recorded your dream in its raw, original form, including as many details as possible, now it's time to write its meaning. If you have an idea of what you believe the dream means, write down your interpretation. But remember, write your interpretation under and separate from your account of the raw dream itself. This is important because your interpretation may change or grow, but the dream itself will not.

As you follow these five simple steps, your ability to remember your dreams will increase dramatically. Then as you review your dream journal from time to time, you will see how God has been using your dreams to guide and strengthen you as you seek to fulfill His destiny for you.

In Closing

The Bible says God is a rewarder of those who diligently seek Him (Heb. 11:6). If you make time for God, He is going to bless you. So, beloved, wake up early and press in to the Lord about your dreams. Tell Him, "God, I value Your voice. I value Your word to me. I value Your instruction to me. I value the fact that You speak to me. I don't want to take Your voice lightly or treat it flippantly. I don't want to just go on with my day. I want to hear what You said and take whatever action is required, to respond in whatever manner is necessary for You to have my full allegiance and for Your word for me to have its full effect."

Beloved, if you believe God speaks in dreams and are asking Him to speak to you as you sleep, He will. How do I know that? I know because dreams are not a gift meant for a select few. Some of the gifts of the Spirit are for certain chosen ones. For example, not everybody operates in the gift of miracles or has the gift of healing. These are specific gifts for specific people for specific times, and the same gifts are not given to everyone. (See Romans 12:4–8 and 1 Corinthians 12:4–13.) But dreams are not gifts for a select number of individuals; they are available to the entire body of believers worldwide and at all times.

Dreams are a means the Father uses to communicate with us, and He wants to communicate with all of His children. Receiving revelation from God through dreams is not just for me, beloved. It is for you too. You need to believe that.

I can't stress it enough—dreams are life changing. When God gives you a dream, it can change you for the better if you'll harvest the meaning. As I close this book, I want to share with you a vivid dream I had early this morning—not to go on and on about my own dreams but to show you how special they can be and how HaShem uses them in our lives.

This morning I woke up at about 4:15 and lay in bed for about two hours, unable to get back to sleep. Finally, I went downstairs to my prayer room and turned on worship music (from ihopkc.org). As I lay on my couch listening to the worship music, I eventually fell back asleep and went into a deep dream state.

In this deep dream state, Cynthia was in the background, and I heard worship music playing. I don't know whether it literally was the worship I was physically listening to or if it was heavenly music of the Spirit, but it was nurturing and caressing my soul.

Next in the dream, a successful businessman came to my front door, and after someone in my home let him in, he took a seat in the room near where I was lying on the couch. As I continued to lay on the couch being ministered to, I glanced up and saw that this businessman sitting in the chair was being ministered to as well. Eventually he left, and I instinctively knew that he had received a spiritual impartation that gave him the strength and health he needed to navigate the busy season into which he was about to enter.

After the businessman left, my daughter appeared in the dream. She is now thirty-one, but in the dream she seemed to be only about twelve to fourteen years old. She had her leg over the backrest of the couch, and it was resting against my cheek. At this stage in the dream, I was just taking in the beauty of my innocent daughter in HaShem's love.

Then my younger daughter appeared in the dream. She is twenty-seven now, but in the dream she appeared to be only seven or eight. In the dream she ran by me, and when she did, she was just so cute, I couldn't resist grabbing her and giving her a little tickle because I love her so much.

In the final part of the dream, I was off the couch and standing in my prayer room when my little dog that has passed away came up to me and rubbed his face against my ankle. (In the dream he was so small that he could only reach my ankle.)

When I woke up, I thought, "Wow, what a dream of being immersed in God's love—hearing and feeling the worship music minister to me and caress my soul, being in the security and intimacy of family, and finally, having my beloved little dog rub his cheek against my ankle, which really touched me."

I immediately recorded the dream. And after I had written it down, I was reminded again why we must be careful about getting locked into our first interpretation of a dream, because what I believe is the full interpretation of the dream did not come until hours later. Here's what I think it meant and why I wanted to share it with you.

I believe the successful businessman in the dream was me, and the Lord was showing me that I was getting ready to enter into another very busy season. But because the

Lord had imparted His shalom—indeed, even Himself—to me in that dream experience, I am now ready to enter into the busy season I know I will be facing. So God prepared me for this upcoming season by imparting Himself to me in the dream and giving me the confidence to know that I am equipped to handle what is coming in the next season because of what He poured into me in the dream.

So why did I share that with you? To teach you how special and important dreams can be for you. As you pay attention to the voice of God through your dreams, He will equip you, train you, and prepare you for your future.

If you've disregarded your dreams, repent. Just say: "Father, forgive me. I haven't paid attention to my dreams the way I should have. I have disregarded Your Spirit speaking to me in my dreams at night, and, Father, I ask for Your forgiveness. I'm going to commit to seeking to understand what You said to me in my dreams the night before. When I wake up in the morning, the first thing I'm going to do is ask You whether You spoke to me in my sleep last night."

There is so much you gain by tuning in to your dreams. That is why in the remainder of this book I have left space for you to write down your dreams. Please seize this opportunity. I believe if you are willing to spend time with the Lord first thing every morning, write down your dreams exactly as they happened, and then pray for the interpretation, you will find that Father God will speak to you powerfully!

Remember—to disregard your dreams is to disregard the voice of God being spoken into your life.

Baruch HaShem, this is Rabbi Schneider saying I love

you, and as we close this section of the book, I want to pray for you.

> *Father God, in Yeshua's name I ask You to remove anything that is blocking this dear one from hearing Your voice. Yeshua, You said, "He that has ears to hear, let them hear what the Spirit has to say." [See Matthew 11:15.]*
>
> *Father, You said what we loose on earth will be loosed in heaven. [See Matthew 18:18.] So, Father, in Yeshua's name I loose the ears of Your people to hear You speaking to them at night. Father, open the ears right now of those who are seeking to hear from You in their dreams. And Satan, I take authority over you, and I break up the blockage you've created over the ears of God's people that has prevented them from hearing from Father God through His Spirit in their dreams at night.*
>
> *Father, right now I ask You to whisper to Your people in their dreams at night. Give them a spirit of wisdom and revelation in the knowledge of You. Father, I ask You to teach Your people how to understand the symbolism in their dreams so they can clearly discern what You're revealing through their dreams. In Yeshua's name, amen.*

PART II

YOUR DREAM JOURNAL

_____

_____

_____

_____

_____

_____

_____

_____

_____

_____

_____

_____

_____

_____

_____

_____

_____

_____

_____

_____

_____

_____

ABOUT THE AUTHOR

MESSIANIC RABBI KIRT A. Schneider, a Jewish believer in Jesus and end-times messenger of the Lord, delivers the word of the Lord with a true passion of the Holy Spirit. When Rabbi Schneider was twenty years old, the Lord suddenly awakened him and revealed Himself as Jesus the Messiah on the cross, and his life has never been the same. He has since pastored, traveled internationally as an evangelist, served as rabbi of a Messianic synagogue, and is currently a *schliach* (messenger) of Jesus the Messiah to the world.

Rabbi Schneider is the host of the international television broadcast *Discovering the Jewish Jesus*, which can be seen seven days a week in more than one hundred million homes in the United States and approximately two hundred nations worldwide. Viewers tune in regularly as Rabbi Schneider shows with exceptional clarity how the Old and New Testaments connect and how Jesus completes the unfolding plan of God. For a list of times and stations that broadcast Rabbi Schneider's program in your area, visit www. DiscoveringTheJewishJesus.com and click on the "Ways to Watch" tab. His program can also be viewed via YouTube.

In addition to hosting mass evangelistic outreaches and broadcasting through television all around the globe, Rabbi Schneider is the author of several books, including *Rivers of Revelation*, *Lion of Judah*, *Experiencing the Supernatural*, *The Book of Revelation Decoded*, and *Awakening to Messiah*. He and his wife, Cynthia, have two children and have been married since 1983.

WWW.DISCOVERINGTHEJEWISHJESUS.COM

DISCOVERING THE JEWISH JESUS

CONNECT
WITH RABBI SCHNEIDER

www.DiscoveringTheJewishJesus.com

 www.facebook.com/rabbischneider

 @RabbiSchneider

 @discoveringthejewishjesus

 https://www.youtube.com/user/
RabbiSchneider

NOTES

INTRODUCTION

1.   "Dreams," WebMD, accessed December 23, 2019, https://www.webmd.com/sleep-disorders/dreaming-overview#1.

2.   Uptin Saiidi, "US Life Expectancy Has Been Declining. Here's Why," CNBC, July 9, 2019, https://www.cnbc.com/2019/07/09/us-life-expectancy-has-been-declining-heres-why.html.

CHAPTER 1: GOD STILL SPEAKS THROUGH DREAMS

1.   Blue Letter Bible, s.v. *"naba',"* accessed December 23, 2019, https://www.blueletterbible.org/lang/Lexicon/Lexicon.cfm?strongs=H5012&t=KJV.

CHAPTER 3: WHERE DREAMS COME FROM

1.   "Devekut," Jewish Virtual Library, accessed December 23, 2019, https://www.jewishvirtuallibrary.org/devekut.